A close look at
the Netherlands

Contents

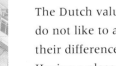

I live in the Netherlands

I live in the Dutch countryside. You can see very far there and the sky is often full of beautiful clouds. I can see all kinds of shapes in them. When I ride my bicycle to school, I don't have to go uphill, because everything is flat. There is a lot of wind, though. When the wind is behind me I can ride nice and fast. But it seems like the wind is usually against me...

Our farm is in a village by the sea. After school I visit my pony. Actually, he belongs to a farmer. But I take care of him and I'm allowed to ride him. When the weather is good, we go galloping across the beach!

On a farm there is always work to do, so we don't go on vacation very often. But we can go on day trips. There are so many fun things to do in the Netherlands. Sometimes we go to a zoo or an amusement park.

Low and flat with lots of water

Frisian Islands

Groningen

Leeuwarden

Assen

Amsterdam

Lelystad

Haarlem

Oostvaardersplassen

Zwolle

North Sea

Schiphol Airport

The Hague

Utrecht

Arnhem

Rotterdam

GERMANY

The Rhine

's-Hertogenbosch

Middelburg

Vlissingen

The Maas

BELGIUM

Vaalserberg

Maastricht

Small and densely populated

The Netherlands is a small country on the North Sea. From any place in the country, the farthest point is never more than 350 kilometres away. It takes only a little more than four hours to travel by train from Vlissingen, in the southwest, to Groningen, in the northeast.

More than 15 million people live there, which makes the Netherlands the most densely populated country in the world. Most of the people in the Netherlands live in the west of the country. That is where the four largest cities, Amsterdam, Rotterdam, The Hague, and Utrecht, are located. Amsterdam is the capital, but The Hague is the seat of government.

The Dutch flag

The Netherlands is sometimes called Holland, because an area in the west of the Netherlands used to be called Holland. The name lives on in the names of two Dutch provinces: North Holland and South Holland. The language spoken in the Netherlands is Dutch. In the province of Friesland, Frisian is also spoken. That is a separate language, which is a little bit like English.

Getting away from the crowds

Even though the Netherlands is densely populated, it has many nature areas and magnificent views. Outside the large, modern cities there are picturesque towns and villages. There is even a nature area in the middle of the busy western part of the country. This area is known as the Green Heart. And all over the Netherlands you can find water, water, and more water. Rivers and canals run through the cities and the countryside. Cows and sheep graze in green meadows and water flows through the ditches that surround them. You can go sailing and windsurfing on the many lakes. On the coast there are broad, sandy beaches, dunes, and popular seaside resorts.

The Netherlands, a low country

The Netherlands is a low-lying country and most of it is flat. Almost a third of the country is below sea level. The lowest point, near Rotterdam, is 6.74 metres below sea level. Dunes, walls of earth called dikes, and other sea walls protect the country from the water. Without them, many areas would be flooded at high tide. The highest point in the Netherlands is at the top of the Vaalserberg, a hill 322 metres high located in the south of the province of Limburg.

Mild weather

The Netherlands has a temperate climate. The winters are mild. In January the average temperature is 2 degrees Celsius. The summers are fairly cool. In July the average temperature is 17 degrees Celsius. But during the summer it can stay warm and sunny for weeks, and temperatures can reach 30 degrees Celsius. In the winter there is sometimes frost or snow, and in both autumn and winter there can be storms and sometimes it is foggy. In the morning there is often mist on the pastures. Sometimes the cows half disappear into the mist. It's an odd sight.

Every cloud has a silver lining

In the Netherlands it can get rainy or windy in any season. The Dutch often complain about the rain and wind. But they also have their advantages. The rain makes the ground fertile, so that vegetables, fruit, and grain can be grown there. The Netherlands is a good place for flowers too. In the spring colourful fields of tulips, carnations, and daffodils draw tourists from all over the world.

The Netherlands is famous for its flowers and bulbs. When spring arrives in the Keukenhof, an enormous flower garden in South Holland, you can see what a variety of beautiful flowers the Netherlands has to offer.

Mills can be built in many different ways. For example, this tower mill has a balcony all round.

▼

Mills even have their own language. The position of the vanes has a specific meaning for people living nearby. When a baby is born or when there is a wedding, the miller will hang little flags or other decorations on them.

Modern windmills are used to generate electricity. Using wind energy helps to conserve the environment.

▼

Harnessing the wind

Centuries ago the Dutch were already using the wind to their own advantage by building windmills. They were used to drain away water and create dry land. Windmills are still used. Some mills grind grain into flour, and others press oil out of seeds, or grind mustard seeds to make mustard. Windmills are also used in making paper and paint, and for sawing wood. At one time there were almost 10,000 mills in the Netherlands. Now only about 1,000 are left.

Nature reserves

The Netherlands is very built up, but there is still enough room for nature reserves with woods and heathland. There are hills and woods in the south of the province of Limburg. The Oostvaardersplassen is a nature area in the province of Flevoland with a great deal of water. It is a paradise for birds. Geese, spoonbills, and cormorants make their nests there.

Another place with many animals is the Veluwe, a nature area with woods and heathland in the middle of the country. If you get an early start, you can see wild boar, red deer, roe deer, and foxes there. Along the coast there are dunes and broad, sandy beaches, where you can see seagulls constantly gliding through the air. The Dutch dunes contain an enormous variety of wildlife. There is a lot more than just sand there; there are also forests, swamps, and ponds. Many unusual plants grow there, such as burnet roses and sea holly. And the dunes are an ideal environment for all kinds of birds.

Many wetland areas offer a wide variety of birds the opportunity to brood in peace. Here you see a colony of cormorants in a watery area.

In the mud flats, waders often find themselves up to their knees in mud.

▼

Wading across the sea

In the north of the Netherlands lie the Frisian Islands. They are made up mainly of dunes and sand, but there are also villages there. Many tourists go there in the summer. Cars are not allowed on some of the islands.

The Waddenzee separates the Frisian Islands from the mainland. At low tide, some shallow mud flats in the Waddenzee almost fall dry. Sometimes, when the weather is good, you can walk from the shore of the mainland all the way across to one of the islands. This is an adventure that is not without risks; you have to make sure you get back on shore before the water rises. For that reason, you have to be accompanied by an experienced guide. Also, you must be at least twelve years old, because slogging through the wet, muddy flats is too tiring for younger children. While wading you can see seals, mussel beds, shells, water birds, and vast panoramas. A couple of hours later the mud flats disappear into the sea again.

A land
of water

In the polders there are farms, pastures, fields, and ditches. The water level is lower in the polder than in the canal that surrounds it.

▼

Polders

The Netherlands is known for its polders. Polders make up almost two-fifths of the country's area. A polder is a stretch of land that lies below sea level and is protected from the water by dikes. The Dutch have built dikes to protect low-lying areas ever since the Middle Ages. Sometimes the dikes broke and the land was flooded. That created large lakes. Later, the Dutch turned these lakes back into polders. The IJsselmeer used to be an inland sea. In 1932 a long dike was built to close it. Polders were made in the lake that was formed. Now there is a great deal of modern farming on those polders, and cities and towns have been built there to provide housing for the steadily growing Dutch population.

Water is carried out of the polders by the ditches that run through them. In the past, windmills moved excess water into the rivers. Nowadays large pumps keep the polders dry.

Public enemy number one – the sea

Making the dikes higher and stronger is still important. In 1996 some of the dikes on the big rivers threatened to burst, because the water level was unusually high. Thousands of people fled their homes. But the dikes held out and after a few days they were able to return.

In 1953, gale force winds and high tides caused the dikes to burst in the province of Zeeland. The islands in the province were flooded. After that, enormous dams and other constructions were built to protect the islands. They were the largest ever built anywhere in the world. It took thirty years to finish them all. This was known as the Delta Project.

Their constant battle with the sea has made the Dutch experts in building dikes, dams, and everything that goes with them. Some large Dutch companies protect the coastline and riverbanks by dredging – clearing away sludge from the bottom of rivers and other waterways – and by reclaiming land – making new land where before there was only water. These companies are active in areas all over the world, such as Asia and the Middle East.

▲

The Eastern Scheldt Storm Surge Barrier is a dam 8 kilometres long. It has 62 openings, which are closed off with sliding barriers at high tide.

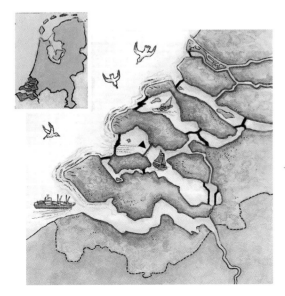

◄ *The Delta works are enormous constructions such as dams (in black) and dikes (in red), for holding back seawater. They protect the southwest of the Netherlands from the sea. The Zeeland Bridge (indicated with an arrow) is part of the Delta works. The bridge is 5 kilometres long. It connects two islands in the province of Zeeland.*

Two big cities

Eva is twelve years old and lives in Amsterdam, the capital of the Netherlands. She can tell you all about her city.

"The centre of Amsterdam is very old. Further out, there are modern flats and office buildings. Canals run through the centre of the city. Along the canals there are stately mansions, and also warehouses that have been turned into homes. Most of these buildings date back to the 16th and 17th century.

"The city centre is built on loose soil. People pounded wooden poles into the earth and put buildings on top of them so that they would not sink into the ground. So in Amsterdam the houses are on stilts!

"The city centre is always busy. You can often hear barrel organs playing in the street. Those are colourful organs on wheels that play music when you turn a crank. There are figures on them that dance to the music. Barrel organs often play well-known tunes. The organ-grinder shakes his cup of coins in time to the music and people give him money.

"Why don't you visit Amsterdam? You can take a boat trip along the canals, or go to the zoo, which is called Artis. Do you like art? Then you should visit the Rijksmuseum sometime! There you can see Rembrandt's 'Night Watch', an extremely large and very famous painting."

◄ *Canals lined with tall houses are characteristic of the centre of Amsterdam.*

Cargo ships from around the world come to the port of Rotterdam. The Maas river connects Rotterdam with inland Europe. But the Maas also divides Rotterdam in half. The Erasmus Bridge is one of the bridges connecting the two halves of the city.

Marco is thirteen years old and lives in Rotterdam. He can also tell you a lot about his city.

"Rotterdam is the world's largest port. The Maas river cuts right through the city. It's a wide river that flows into the sea. There are always boats of all sizes sailing on it. There's not much left of the old city centre in Rotterdam. It was destroyed in the Second World War. After the war a whole new city was built. In the centre there are tall office buildings, a large shopping centre and modern bridges across the Maas. Close to the river are strange buildings that look like cubes. And behind them is an old building with a pointy red roof that we call 'the pencil'. We also call the newest bridge 'the swan'. We're good at making up nicknames here in Rotterdam! There's a lot to see and do. Every year there's an international film festival. There are famous museums here and a lot of festivals and pop concerts. I just visited our zoo, Blijdorp. The animals' natural habitats have been recreated so carefully that they almost seem real."

Every inch counts

The Netherlands is a small country with a lot of people in it. Many different solutions have been thought up for the shortage of space. For example, at busy intersections highways are often stacked one above the other. And one of the runways at Amsterdam's Schiphol Airport has been built over a road, to save space. Seeing such a gigantic aeroplane right in front of your car is pretty impressive.

Caring for the environment

The Netherlands is known as a clean country. A great deal is done to fight pollution from industry, agriculture and traffic. Factories must follow strict rules. And many vegetable and fruit growers use insects like ladybirds and bumblebees instead of poisons to get rid of weeds and pests. Dutch people are using more and more special detergents that are not harmful to the environment. Many people have a separate waste bin for vegetable scraps. Near the shops there are waste bins for glass, paper, and clothing. All these materials are recycled. The government encourages people to use their bicycles more often or take public transport to work, and leave their cars at home.

2 The Dutch in person

Don't fight about it, talk it over

"Just be normal, that's crazy enough," is a favourite Dutch expression. The Dutch are down to earth; they don't like it when people put on airs. Freedom is important to them. And they are used to standing up for themselves and their ideas. Centuries ago the Dutch were already making agreements with each other about things like taxes and new laws. After all, in a densely populated country like the Netherlands, agreement is very important. Dutch people prefer to settle disagreements by talking rather than fighting.

Prosperity and busy streets

The Dutch have a knack for trading and doing business that has made the Netherlands a prosperous country. You can tell when you see the well-dressed people in the street and the wide range of merchandise in supermarkets, department stores, or other shops. Many people leave for work early in the morning. They travel by car, bicycle, train, tram, bus, and metro. In the morning every kind of public transport is packed. And it is packed again in the evening, since most businesses close at five o'clock.

The bicycle is an important way of getting around in the Netherlands. There are separate cycle tracks alongside the roads. Many children ride their bicycles to school. And it is quite normal to see a mayor or a professor cycling to work.

In the Netherlands there are more bicycles than people. Almost everybody has at least one bicycle. In crowded cities you can get around faster by bicycle than by car. And riding a bicycle is better for the environment.

The Dutch at home

For most of the year it is too cold to sit outside in the Netherlands, and people spend most of the time indoors. So having a pleasant, comfortable place to live is very important to the Dutch. They take good care of their homes and put a lot of effort into furnishing and decorating them. Their houses look clean and tidy, just like the streets.

Out in the country there are lots of farms. Each region has its own type of farm. In old farmhouses the walls above the fireplace and in the kitchen are often decorated with ceramic tiles. Especially around the cities there are many tall blocks of flats. In the past few years many new housing estates have been built as well. The houses have gardens, and there are canals and public squares. This new housing was needed because the population has greatly increased. In 1900, the number of people living in the Netherlands was only a third of what it is now.

Old houses and houseboats

Many people like to live in old houses. The authorities protect some of them. They are historic buildings, and must stay the way they are. In the Zaanse Schans, an area to the north of Amsterdam with a lot of water, there is an entire neighbourhood of wooden houses and mills which were built in the 17th century. Many tourists come to see them. Most of them have beautiful gardens.

Some people in the Netherlands live on the water in houseboats. There are many houseboats on Amsterdam's canals. Some look like modern houses with large windows; others look more like ordinary boats. They have electricity and telephones, just like ordinary houses. Many houseboats are not really boats any more, because they can no longer set sail.

◀ *Houses with peaked roofs and red roof tiles are typically Dutch.*

Obviously, you cannot have a garden on a houseboat, so the people who live in them often put potted plants out on their decks or have a small garden on shore.

▼

Home is where the heart is

Since the Dutch spend quite a lot of time at home, they put a lot of time and money into furnishing and decorating their houses. It doesn't matter whether you prefer the contemporary or the old-fashioned look, as long as your home is attractive and comfortable. In most Dutch houses there are plants and flowers on the windowsills, cupboards, and tables. In the evenings many people leave the curtains open. That makes it easy to look inside. But don't stand in front of the window staring for too long. Dutch people consider that very rude.

De Jordaan is an old district in Amsterdam. In the early 20th century three families would be crowded into each house there. Families were much bigger then than they are now. The children even had to sleep in the kitchen.

Free time

All children may join the library free of charge.

Many Dutch people belong to a sports club, a theatre group, a musical society, or a choir. The Netherlands has more choirs than any other country in the world. Others use their free time for learning. They might study a foreign language or learn to cook or paint, for instance.

Dutch people spend a lot of time doing jobs in and around their homes. They do carpentry, paint, and work in the garden. At the weekend they often visit family or friends.

The Netherlands is truly a land of flowers. Many flowers grow there and you can buy them everywhere – in fancy flower shops, at flower stalls on the street, and even at filling stations or supermarkets. It is a Dutch custom to bring along flowers when visiting someone.

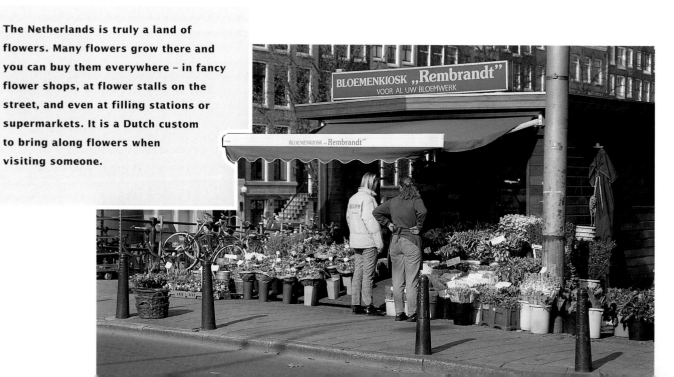

When the weather is good, most children play outside. They play football, get on their skateboards, or put on their in-line skates.

▼

23

Many people watch television in the evening. In most places you can receive many different stations, including foreign ones. Foreign programmes are often shown on Dutch television. These programmes are subtitled; at the bottom of the screen you can read in Dutch what the people are saying. Dutch people usually speak at least one foreign language.

Vacation

Many Dutch people go on vacation once a year, and some go more than once. Often they go abroad. But they also enjoy the sun, the beach, and the sea in their own country. On weekends cyclists and hikers head for nature areas. When the weather is good, tens of thousands of people come to the beaches to enjoy the sun and the sea.

Sports

Most Dutch people know how to swim. Children learn when they are still young; many children already know how to swim before they turn six. It is a necessary skill in a country with so much water. Besides, most children like to swim.

Sports are an important free-time activity. Football is an especially popular game, both to play and to watch. Hardly anybody wants to miss the television

broadcasts of major international championships. When an important match is on, the streets are practically empty, and thousands of fans go to see the Dutch team play abroad. You can recognise Dutch fans by their orange caps and clothing. Dutch footballers such as Johan Cruijff, Ruud Gullit and Dennis Bergkamp are famous all over the world.

Winter and summer sports

Skating

Skating is one of the best-loved sports in the Netherlands. Every winter people hope it will get cold enough to make thick natural ice that they can skate on. When that time comes, half the country takes off to the lakes and canals. Men, women, and children – everyone bundles up and heads out onto the ice. Schools sometimes give children a day off in icy weather. Skating clubs organise marathons. Everyone has a good time and there are stands where you can buy soup, coffee, hot chocolate, and cake.

The Elfstedentocht

When the temperature has been well below zero for a long time and the ice is at least 15 centimetres thick, it is time for the Elfstedentocht, a skating marathon, held in Friesland. This exhausting 200-kilometre tour through 11 Frisian towns is practically a national holiday. People come to Friesland from near and far to cheer on the 2,000 or so skaters who take part. Others follow the tour on television.

Many skaters never reach the finishing line. Whoever does is given a hero's welcome. It is not often cold enough to hold the Elfstedentocht.

During the Elfstedentocht the skaters are warmly dressed. The tour takes them under many bridges like this one. There are always people standing on the bridges to cheer them on.

Sailing

In the summer all the lakes and rivers turn into water again. When the wind is right, it is time for sailing. International sailing competitions are held on the Frisian lakes. One of the most spectacular competitions is the skûtsjesilen race. Skûtsjes are large, flat cargo ships with sails, built between 1900 and 1930. Their crews have their work cut out for them just keeping the boat under control, especially in bad weather. It is fantastic to see the ships trying to overtake one another. The races have been compared to sea battles without the fighting.

Traditional costume

You sometimes see pictures of the Dutch in traditional costume; the men are dressed in baggy pants and wooden shoes and the women wear a long skirt and a bonnet. Many country people used to dress this way. Now you only see traditional costume in a few villages. On the coast of the IJsselmeer and in the province of Zeeland traditional costume is still worn, especially by older people. Wooden shoes used to be worn by people who worked in the fields. They are nice and warm and easy to scuff clean at the front door, so that you do not track mud all over the house.

Food and drink

For breakfast and lunch, most Dutch people eat sandwiches. In the evening they eat a hot meal, which often includes potatoes. Between meals the Dutch generally drink coffee and tea. The biscuit tin is always full, since many Dutch people have a sweet tooth; liquorice and chocolate are also favourites.

Many cultures

People from many different countries and cultures live in the Netherlands, especially in the cities, where you come across many different skin colours as well as foreign languages and exotic clothing. The Netherlands has always welcomed foreigners. For centuries people persecuted for their religion or political beliefs in their own country have taken refuge there.

Indonesian festivals are held all over the country. The largest is the Pasar Malam in The Hague. People meet there once a year to enjoy delicious food and music from their homeland.

Foreigners have also come to the Netherlands for other reasons. Indonesia, a country in Southeast Asia, and Suriname, a country in South America, used to be Dutch territories. A lot of people from those countries took Dutch nationality or married Dutch people. When the two countries became independent, many of them came to the Netherlands. The Netherlands Antilles, two groups of islands in the Caribbean, still belong to the Netherlands. People also come to the Netherlands from there.

Other immigrants came from Italy, Spain, Morocco, and Turkey when there were a lot of jobs in the Netherlands. Many of them decided to stay. These immigrants brought along their own culture and traditions. They started their own shops and restaurants, where other Dutch people also like to go. They also built places of worship so they could practise their own religions.

95% Dutch
5% Other nationalities

32% Catholic   3.7% Moslem
22% Protestant   42.3% Other or no religion

3 A rich past...and present!

The good old days

The first inhabitants

There were people living in the Netherlands 250,000 years ago. We know that because we have dug up some of the tools they used. Most of the tools that have been found are celts, sharpened stones that resemble axes. Celts were used for all sorts of things, like modern-day pocket knives. The people who used them had no metal objects.

Romans

In the year 55 B.C., Roman troops occupied the south of the Netherlands. The Romans stayed for several hundred years. They built roads and bridges, villas, and bathhouses, and founded cities such as Maastricht and Nijmegen.

The Golden Age

In the Middle Ages trade became more and more important and the towns grew. The 17th century (1600-1700) was a time of great prosperity. That is why we call this century the Golden Age. A lot of wonderful art and literature was created, and important discoveries were made. Dutch merchants made big profits from overseas trading. They would travel to faraway lands in ships laden with gold and silver and buy products there that were unavailable in the Netherlands: spices, such as pepper, cinnamon, nutmeg, and cloves, and other merchandise, including silk, cotton, china, coffee, tea, and sugar.

You can tell times were good in the Netherlands during the Golden Age when you see the beautiful houses that were built for merchants and other wealthy people. Many of these houses line Amsterdam's canals. The tops of the housefronts, called gables, were built in a wide variety of styles. The simplest kind of gable slants upward. There are also gables shaped like staircases and bells, as well as narrow bottleneck gables with decorative carvings on both sides. Try to spot all these kinds of gable in the drawing below.

Many merchants grew rich from overseas trade. They had luxurious houses built just outside Amsterdam.

The Dutch East India Company

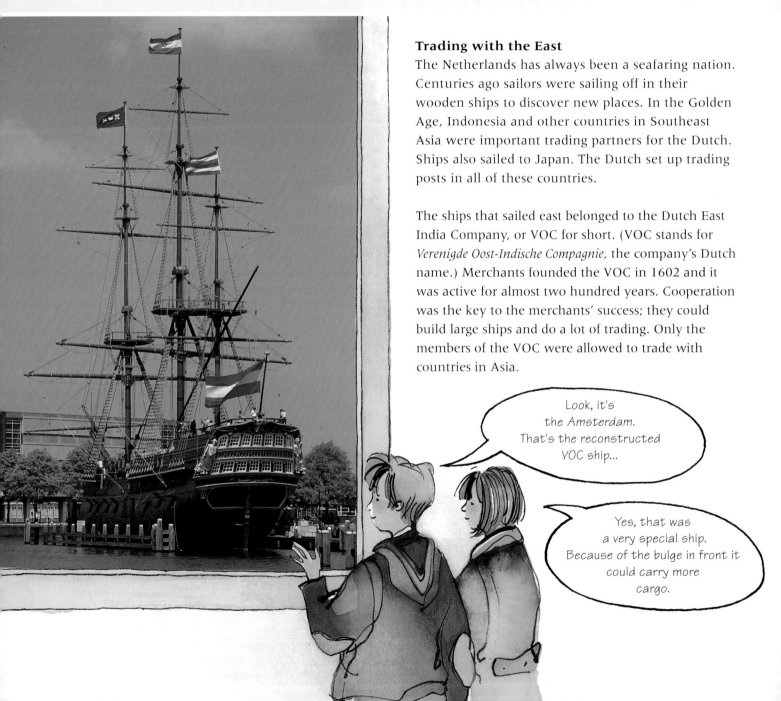

Trading with the East

The Netherlands has always been a seafaring nation. Centuries ago sailors were sailing off in their wooden ships to discover new places. In the Golden Age, Indonesia and other countries in Southeast Asia were important trading partners for the Dutch. Ships also sailed to Japan. The Dutch set up trading posts in all of these countries.

The ships that sailed east belonged to the Dutch East India Company, or VOC for short. (VOC stands for *Verenigde Oost-Indische Compagnie*, the company's Dutch name.) Merchants founded the VOC in 1602 and it was active for almost two hundred years. Cooperation was the key to the merchants' success; they could build large ships and do a lot of trading. Only the members of the VOC were allowed to trade with countries in Asia.

Look, it's the Amsterdam. That's the reconstructed VOC ship...

Yes, that was a very special ship. Because of the bulge in front it could carry more cargo.

The VOC was founded as a peaceful organisation. Its goal was to trade with foreign countries, not to conquer them. However, the ships were equipped with cannons, and soldiers often came along to protect the ship and its valuable cargo from pirates and other enemies.

On board a VOC ship

Imagine you are in 17th-century Amsterdam. A drum roll fills the street. A town crier announces that ten ships are setting sail for the East. They need sailors. Men and boys are called on to sign up. Would you go along? In those days many boys signed up as sailors, cooks, or barbers. They were happy to have the work and their lives were full of adventure. Back then, going to sea was the only way to learn about foreign countries first-hand. Women were not allowed to go along. However, girls did manage to sneak on board sometimes by disguising themselves as boys.

Life on board was not easy. The insides of the ships were fairly small. The officers were given their own rooms, but the sailors had to find places to sleep for themselves. If they were unlucky, they ended up spending the night out in the cold on deck. The outward journey alone took eight to ten months, because the ships had to sail all the way around the southern tip of Africa.

Some of the ships sank when the weather turned bad. Many of them have been found on the bottom of the ocean. Some of them still contain gold or valuable china, as well as everyday things like drinking cups, pipes, shoes, cherry pits, bottles of wine and cans of cheese and tobacco.

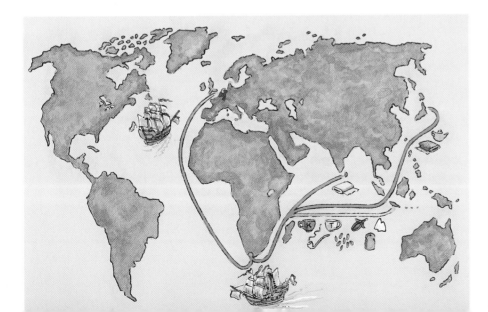

china
silk
cotton
coffee
tea
cocoa
sugar
tobacco
rice
spices:
cinnamon
nutmeg
cloves
pepper

The Kingdom of the Netherlands

The third Tuesday in September is the day the Queen rides through The Hague to Parliament in a coach, known as the golden coach because it is covered with gold leaf. It is an important day in the Netherlands, because it marks the beginning of a new year for the Dutch government.
The Queen announces the government's plans for the coming year.

The Dutch parliament assembles in The Hague.

William of Orange

The Netherlands is a monarchy. At its head is a king or queen. The Royal House is also known as the House of Orange, after Queen Beatrix's most famous ancestor, Prince William of Orange. He was born in 1533 and died in 1584. William of Orange meant so much to the Netherlands that he became known as the father of his country. He was a wise and quiet man, who weighed his words carefully. This earned him the name of 'William the Silent'. He fought for freedom of religion and freedom of expression. And he certainly made history. Today, the Netherlands is a peace-loving nation where people stand up for what they believe in and practise whatever religion they wish.

The Queen and the ministers

The Queen is the head of state, but she does not make any decisions on her own. The government is made up of the Queen and the ministers. The Queen signs all the new laws, which are written by the ministers. Parliament makes sure the government does its job well.

Members of Parliament represent the Dutch people. Every four years they are democratically elected. That means that all Dutch citizens are allowed to vote. Many other countries do not have a king or queen. Instead, they have a president who is chosen directly by the people. The office of king or queen is passed on from parent to child.

William of Orange

34

The Royal House

Queen Beatrix

Queen Beatrix is married to Claus van Amsberg, who was born in Germany. Beatrix and Claus have three sons: Willem-Alexander, born in 1967; Johan Friso, born in 1968; and Constantijn, born in 1969. As the eldest son, Willem-Alexander will succeed his mother on the throne. It is not yet known when he will become king.

The Queen spends the entire week in meetings with ministers and people from provinces, cities, and all kinds of organisations. She has to approve and sign the laws passed by the government. She also has to go on a lot of visits, both within the Netherlands and abroad. In addition, she opens special exhibitions, gives out important prizes, and receives ambassadors and heads of state from foreign countries.

Prince Willem-Alexander

Prince Willem-Alexander studied history. He mainly studied subjects that will be useful when he becomes king. But he also learned to pilot aeroplanes. Willem-Alexander loves sports. He is often present at important sporting events. Once he even skated the Elfstedentocht. When he got to the finish, his mother was waiting for him on the ice.

On 30 April, her official birthday, Queen Beatrix visits different places in the Netherlands. Wherever she goes, she is greeted with enthusiasm.

▼

"Up with Orange!" Dutch sports fans also wear orange. When Dutch teams play abroad, you can tell where the Dutch fans are sitting by the colour of their clothes.

The Queen's Birthday

30 April is the official Queen's Birthday. Queen Beatrix was born on 31 January, but she celebrates on her mother's birthday. The Dutch people celebrate with her. Many people dress up in orange clothing and carry around orange balloons. People decorate their bicycles, their houses, and their babies' prams. Flags are flown with the orange pennant, the symbol of the House of Orange. Hundreds of thousands of people go to Amsterdam, Utrecht, or another city to visit the open flea market. Throughout the city centre the streets are filled with people trying to sell things – knick-knacks, food, books, T-shirts, or whatever they want to get rid of. Some children play games; others show off their musical talents.

Famous Dutch people

Books

Anne Frank Anne Frank's diary has made her world famous. Anne was a Jewish girl who had to go into hiding with her family during the Second World War. From 1942 on, the family lived in hiding in the back of a house alongside a canal in Amsterdam. The house still exists. Thousands of people visit it every year.

Anne died in a concentration camp. After the war her diary was published. It has been translated into lots and lots of languages. Every year on 4 May, all the people who died in the war are commemorated. On 5 May the Dutch celebrate their liberation.

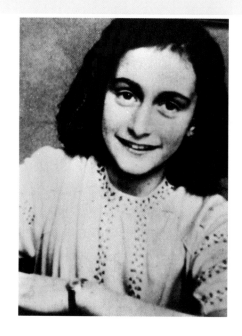

Dick Bruna Dick Bruna is a well-known Dutch author and illustrator of children's books. He has written and illustrated many books for small children. The most famous character in his books is Miffy the rabbit. His drawings are very simple and brightly coloured. Dick Bruna's books have been translated into more than thirty languages.

Of course, many other Dutch authors have written children's books. Maybe someday you will read a book by Thea Beckman, Guus Kuijer, or Carry Slee.

Music

Many Dutch people make music in their free time. More than 400,000 people sing in choirs, for example, and orchestras and pop groups often perform in concert halls and stadiums.

Inventions

Through the centuries, many famous inventions have originated in the Netherlands. Christiaan Huygens (1629-1695) was a scientist during the Golden Age. He became famous for inventing the pendulum clock. That is a kind of clock that is driven by the regular back-and-forth movement of a pendulum. Antonie van Leeuwenhoek (1632-1723) invented the microscope. He made 500 of them, with copper or silver plates and lenses he ground himself. He also discovered bacteria, creatures too small to be seen with the naked eye. The CD, a modern invention, also comes from the Netherlands. The electronics company Philips put the first CDs on the market in 1982.

Every year many artists perform in Feijenoord Stadium in Rotterdam. Dutch and foreign artists draw large audiences.

The Royal Dutch Concertgebouw Orchestra is one of the most famous orchestras in the world and often tours abroad.

Painting

Paintings by Dutch artists can be found in museums all over the world. The prosperous Golden Age (1600-1700) was an especially important period for Dutch art. But there are many important painters from later periods too. Some of the best known are Rembrandt van Rijn, Jan Steen, Johannes Vermeer, Vincent van Gogh, Piet Mondrian, and Karel Appel.

Rembrandt van Rijn   Rembrandt van Rijn (1606-1669) may be the greatest painter of the Golden Age. He was the son of a miller and he lived and worked in Amsterdam. His house is still there and has been turned into a museum. Rembrandt was famous in the Netherlands and abroad during his own lifetime. 'The Night Watch' is one of his best-known paintings. You can see it in the Rijksmuseum in Amsterdam.

Jan Steen is most famous for his paintings of groups of people laughing, singing, and making merry in untidy living rooms. When they see a messy place, Dutch people often say it reminds them of Jan Steen's house.

This is one of Van Gogh's many paintings. It shows a farmer's wife at work.

▼

Vincent van Gogh   Vincent van Gogh (1853-1890) lived and worked in the Netherlands, Belgium, and France. He did not start painting until late in his life. Within ten years he became a great artist. He has a very special style all his own. His paintings and drawings are admired all over the world. Many of his works are in the Netherlands. There is a special museum in Amsterdam with paintings by Van Gogh.

Karel Appel   Karel Appel was born in 1921. In the fifties he shocked some people with his brightly coloured paintings. He used thick layers of paint and you could not even see what they were paintings of. Appel emptied entire tubes of paint onto the canvas. Sometimes he even threw the paint on. But Appel's paintings became world famous and he won many international prizes. When a journalist asked him how he painted, he said, "I just mess around".

This painting, 'Cyclist at Night', is a good example of Karel Appel's colourful style.

▶

4 Farming, trade and industry

Farming, trade and industry

For many years the Dutch have made their living from the products their land had to offer them. Farming, market gardening, fishing, and livestock breeding were (and still are) important ways of earning money. But it is above all trade and industry that have made the Netherlands the wealthy country it is today. In the last hundred years, a lot of factories, roads, and office buildings have been constructed on what used to be farmland. In addition to farming, trade and industry, the service sector is also very important. Many people work for the government, banks, or public transport companies, for example.

Natural resources

The Netherlands has many natural resources under its soil, such as coal, petroleum and natural gas. But it has few of the other natural resources needed by industry. So ever since the rise of industry in the 19th century, they have been imported and processed. The finished products are then sold to countries all over the world. Processing raw materials is one of the Netherlands' greatest strengths. Near Rotterdam there are enormous oil refineries. At night they are so brightly lit that they look like a city. And the fishing village of IJmuiden is the home of Hoogovens Steelworks, which turns pig iron into sheets of steel. These are used to make other products, such as boats and pipes.

Gas and salt

Around 1960 a large pocket of natural gas was discovered underground in the north of the Netherlands. Dutch families use natural gas to cook and to heat their homes. The Netherlands has so much natural gas that it even sells some to other countries.

Salt is another of the Netherlands' natural resources. In 1886 the company Akzo Nobel opened up new salt mines in the east of the country. Since then the company has grown tremendously. Akzo Nobel uses the salt it mines to make table salt, salt for icy roads, and chlorine. The company also makes synthetic fibres for clothing, and paint.

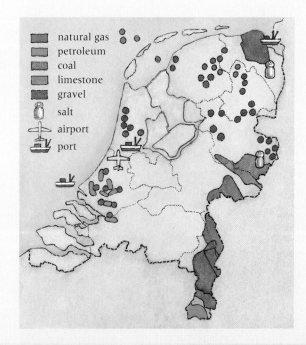

natural gas
petroleum
coal
limestone
gravel
salt
airport
port

Agriculture

The farmer – a modern businessman

There is a great deal of industry in the Netherlands. Only half of the country's surface area is still used for farming, gardening, and livestock breeding. Vegetables, fruit, grain, potatoes, and other crops are grown in both fields and greenhouses. The pastures are filled with grazing cattle and there are large sties where many pigs are kept. Farmers have become modern businessmen. They use modern agricultural machinery which is controlled by computers.

The glass city

Many plants are grown in greenhouses.
In the Westland between Rotterdam and The Hague there are so many greenhouses that the area is known as the glass city. Tomatoes, cucumbers, lettuce, and peppers are the most important crops, but flowers and grapes are also grown there. The temperature and humidity are regulated by computer systems. Fewer modern pesticides and herbicides are used. Instead, vegetable growers use

ladybirds, for instance, which eat smaller insects that are bad for the plants. Sometimes they even bring in snakes to chase away mice.

Flowers and bulbs

The Netherlands is famous for its flowers. Every year thousands of tourists come to see the flowers growing in the bulb fields. But the growers are most interested in the bulbs, not the flowers. Tulip, daffodil, and hyacinth bulbs are sold in countries all over the world.

The flower auction in Aalsmeer is buzzing with activity day and night. The flowers are transported to and from the auction in carts.

An enormous flower shop

Almost two-thirds of all the imported flowers in the world come from the Netherlands. Most of them are sold in Aalsmeer, at the world's largest flower auction. Nowhere else in the Netherlands can you see so many flowers and plants together in one place. The long rows of carts filled with flowers look like a big colourful painting. Roses, tulips, and carnations sell best of all. It smells wonderful there. After the flowers have been sold, they are transported to locations in the Netherlands and abroad. The trucks and aeroplanes that transport the flowers are fitted with cooling systems, so that they stay fresh. Some kinds of bulbs are even frozen so that they can be transported more easily.

Many spring flowers are used for floral parades. The floats are usually decorated with flowers of many different colours which make up a picture or shape.

Dairy delights

Making milk

Cows are raised mainly for their milk. One cow produces about 20 litres of milk a day. Cows are fed and milked by machines. The milk is taken to large dairy plants, where it is purified and put into cardboard containers. It is also used to make butter, cheese, yoghurt, and *kwark*, a kind of cream cheese.

Cheese of all kinds

Every year the Netherlands exports 55 million kilogrammes of cheese. Cheeses from Edam and Gouda are the best known abroad. Dutch cheeses have different 'ages'. The younger the cheese, the milder the flavour. Mature cheese, which has ripened for at least ten months, has a firm texture and a strong flavour.

The cheese market

The most important market for Dutch cheese is in Alkmaar, a town in North Holland which has been selling cheese for more than 600 years. Every week 30,000 kilogrammes of cheese are brought in and sold there.

Cheese trading in Alkmaar has changed very little over the years. First the cheese is tasted and evaluated. Men in white suits and brightly coloured hats stack up the cheeses neatly on colourful handbarrows. Then they run across the market square with the cheeses. The hard part is making sure none of them fall off.

Fishing

Every May, on the day before the fishing boats put out to sea to begin the new season, it is party time in the harbours. The boats are decorated with strings of little flags.

Fishing in the sea

The Netherlands is on the sea. So it is no surprise that fishing is so important there. Dutch fishermen catch many different kinds of fish. In the Netherlands, plaice, cod, whiting, and sole are the fish eaten most. For many Dutch fish lovers, salted herring is a real treat. This is raw herring pickled in brine according to a traditional recipe.

If this herring is delivered fresh from the sea, it is called new Dutch herring. Every year the fishermen in the herring fleet compete to be the first to sail into Scheveningen harbour with a ship full of it. The first barrel brought in is given a special welcome and sold at a high price.

On the street there are little stands where herring is sold. You can dip the herring in chopped onions. To eat it, you tip your head back and slowly lower it into your mouth. You can also eat herring on white bread, or have it cut up into pieces that you can put on cocktail sticks.

Many ways to get there

Amsterdam's Schiphol
Airport is the home of KLM
Royal Dutch Airlines, which
has been around longer
than any other airline in
the world.

A great location

The Netherlands is well located in relation to other countries. Because three large rivers – the Rhine, the Scheldt, and the Maas – flow into the sea there, many products can be transported by water. More than a quarter of Europe's seaborne cargo comes into Rotterdam's docks.

The Netherlands also has a large network of roads and railways, and it has airports. Amsterdam's Schiphol Airport is the largest airport in the Netherlands, and the fourth largest in Europe. It is a modern, international airport. In 1998 more than 27 million passengers used Schiphol Airport, almost twice as many as the number of people in the Netherlands.

The largest port in the world

The port of Rotterdam is the largest in the world. It is made up of many large and small docks. The dock area has been expanded by turning part of the North Sea into dry land. Every day ships sail into the port with products such as petroleum, grain, ore, and coal. More than half of their cargo goes on to other countries. Some of the cargo that comes into the port is stored there to be resold. The rest is loaded onto other ships or trucks.

Europort

The western part of Rotterdam's port is called Europort. Many oil refineries are located there. They turn crude oil, which oil tankers bring to the port from faraway places, into petrol, heating oil, and other kinds of fuel. There are also chemical plants and companies that store and resell oil, ore, and grain. It is an impressive spectacle, especially at night, when the area becomes a jungle of lights.

Cooperation with other European countries

The Netherlands carries out a great deal of trade with other countries in Europe. It is a member of the European Union (the EU for short). The EU is made up of fifteen European countries. They make many kinds of agreements so that is is easier for them to trade with one another. But the EU also works on many other issues. For example, it wants toys to meet the same safety standards in all the countries that belong to it, so that the same ones can be sold everywhere.

Many products are shipped in containers, which are then stacked up on deck.

Household names

All over the world, Dutch companies help to protect coastlines and riverbanks by dredging and by reclaiming land. ▶

The Dutch conquerors

A few Dutch companies have grown immensely during the 20th century. Philips Electronics, where the CD was invented, started out as a light bulb factory in 1892. Now it does business in many different countries. Heineken's first brewery was in Amsterdam but today the company brews beer all over the world. And Unilever, which was set up in 1801, has grown to become one of the world's largest producers of detergents and food. The detergent you use to wash your clothes may well come from Unilever in Rotterdam.

Scientific research

Many Dutch companies are doing very well. This is because there are people who keep trying to develop new products and technologies. A great deal of advanced scientific research is done in the Netherlands, especially at the universities. For example Wageningen Agricultural University is known for its research into new agricultural methods and Delft University of Technology does mainly engineering research.

There is also a large national research centre in the Netherlands, which does research in many different areas: the environment, nutrition, health, and new construction methods, just to name a few. Major Dutch companies carry out their own research as well.

The large Dutch manufacturers are not the only ones with big names. Small businesses also make products that are well-known in other countries. Wooden shoes, for example, are a favourite among tourists. Another popular item is delftware, which is made in Delft, an old city to the west of Rotterdam. Vases, plates, tiles, and other objects are decorated with hand-painted designs and then fired. Sometimes the designs show flowers and birds, and sometimes old-fashioned Dutch or Chinese scenes.

▲
In the Volvo factory in Born, cars are put together by robots.

Industry brings new business
Because of all the industry and trading in the Netherlands, other kinds of companies also do well here. There are large insurance companies, transport concerns, consulting firms, and computer companies.

milk

croissant

apple syrup

muesli

currant bun

orange juice

coffee

tea

peanut butter

margarine

chocolate sprinkles

bread

rusk

jam

cheese

Up on time and off to school

First breakfast, then off on your bike

Janneke is ten years old. She lives in the country. Her father runs a garden centre. Her mother also works for the family business. Janneke gets up at six-thirty and at seven it's time for breakfast with the whole family – Mum, Dad, Janneke and her sister. Janneke starts with a bowl of cornflakes, then has a slice of brown bread with cheese.

Janneke leaves for school early. There is no Catholic school in her village, so she goes to a school in the city. She cycles there with other children. In bad weather, Janneke's father or mother will drive her to school. Dutch schoolchildren do not wear uniforms. Janneke has on jeans and a warm sweater. She also puts on a windjammer. In her backpack she has a lunch box with sandwiches and an apple in it. No meals are served at Dutch schools.

Handing out treats on your birthday

Joost lives in Amsterdam. His school is close to home and his school day starts at eight-thirty. So he does not have to get up until seven-thirty. Then he takes a shower and gets dressed. Today is a special day for Joost – his birthday. When he comes into the living room, he sees that it has been decorated with colourful streamers and balloons. And there is a sign on his chair that says "Joost is 11 years old. Happy Birthday!". Next to his plate there are two presents. The first is a computer game, and the second a pair of football boots. And his brother has drawn a picture for him.

Joost takes a large box to school with him. It has bags of crisps in it. At school he treats all 30 pupils in his class to a bag. And all the teachers get one too.

A day at school

Because schoolchildren often have to work together, in many classrooms the desks are arranged in groups.

Lessons and breaks

Janneke's school day also starts at eight-thirty. It begins with a group discussion of the Children's Newsround of the night before. After that the children usually have an arithmetic or a Dutch lesson. At ten-thirty there is a fifteen-minute break. Then the children play outside. After the break they have geography, history, or biology. In most Dutch primary schools the children are assigned to groups that stay together all day. Every group has its own teacher, who teaches almost every subject.

At twelve-fifteen the children eat their sandwiches at home or at school. After that they play outside until one o'clock. They play all kinds of games, like marbles, skipping, ball, and tag.

Most children have pocket money. Some of them use it to buy themselves a treat, like licorice or marshmallows. Janneke gets three guilders a week pocket money. That is enough to buy two cans of pop. But she is saving a lot of it up for riding boots.

More lessons in the afternoon

After lunch Janneke's school day goes on. So does Joost's. His starts up again at one o'clock. In the afternoon, the children study language or arithmetic, or they have a music class, physical education, or swimming lessons. Sometimes they put on plays. Their parents lend a hand once in a while. They might help the children learn to read or talk to them about road safety.

At Joost's school the children also take English lessons. And there are two computers in the classroom. The children take turns using them. In Joost's classroom there is an arithmetic program on the computers and a program for learning the names of places. Today it is Joost and Jeroen's turn to use the computers. They work on arithmetic, doing sums with fractions and percentages.

Sometimes the class visits a museum or a library. And once a year the pupils go on a school outing or a camping trip. In a couple of weeks, Joost's class will go camping in the woods for three days. They will go there on their bicycles, and some of their

▲

Children in the eighth year of primary school. They are about 12 years old. Dutch children start school at the age of 4. When they are 12, they go on to secondary school.

parents and teachers will go along. They will do all sorts of fun things there, like going on treasure hunts and building campfires. The younger pupils will go on a day trip to the zoo and the playground.

After school

A typical Dutch meal

Janneke's school finishes at half past three. She cycles straight home. A farmer in her village has ponies. Janneke takes care of one of them and is allowed to ride it. Janneke also likes to help make supper. Between six and seven her family generally eats a traditional Dutch supper, which often includes potatoes. Some typical Dutch dishes are pea soup and kale with sausage. Janneke loves *hutspot*, which is mashed potatoes with onions, carrots, and stewed beef stirred in.

Homework and a party

Joost's mother is a teacher at a Protestant *gymnasium*, which is a kind of grammar school where the students take Greek and Latin and prepare for university. When Joost gets home at four o' clock, his mother is often there already. They drink tea together and tell each other what they did that day. After that Joost does his homework or plays games on his computer. Sometimes he watches a children's programme on television. Children Janneke and Joost's age do not get a lot of homework. Sometimes they have to study geography, prepare for a test, or finish some of their schoolwork. The only thing that takes more time is working on a project or presentation.

In the last year of primary school, when they turn twelve, children all over the country take a special test. Their teachers look at the results so they can decide what kind of secondary school each child should go to.

Joost has Wednesday afternoons off. So he has plenty of time to have fun playing football or visiting friends. Once a week he has a saxophone lesson at a music school.

Today Joost's friends are coming over after school for his birthday party. They play games and drink pop. There are eleven candles on the cake, and everybody gets a piece. At the end of the party Joost's mother makes *poffertjes*, which are little pancakes. That night there are even more visitors for Joost. His grandfather and grandmother, aunts and uncles, and friends of his parents celebrate his birthday with coffee and cake. And of course, Joost is very curious about the presents he will get!

Vacations and other outings

A thrilling day out

Dutch parents almost always go on vacation with their children. Many Dutch families spend their vacations abroad, in Germany, France, Spain, or some place even farther away. Joost went skiing in Austria this year.

Janneke's father runs his own business, so he cannot go away for very long. In the summer her family rents a house on the beach, not far from home. They also take day trips and go to children's plays when there is a children's theatre group performing in the city, or children's movies at the cinema.

Sometimes Janneke goes to the Efteling with her parents. The Efteling is the best-known amusement park in the Netherlands. There is a big forest there where fairy tales practically come to life. Janneke used to get excited about visiting the enchanted forest. But now that she is a little older, she prefers more adventurous activities. And there are plenty of those in the park as well. For example, you can take a voyage of discovery on a fast-moving water slide. You are carried along by a raging river with waterfalls, rapids, and steep cliffs. Janneke also really likes the giant roller coaster.

◀ *The Efteling is an amusement park. It has been around for a while, but it has the latest, most exciting attractions.*

If you want to get a good idea of what the Netherlands is like and you don't have much time, you should visit the miniature city of Madurodam in The Hague. There you can see models of houses, harbours, and neighbourhoods from all over the Netherlands.

Visiting the tropics in the Netherlands

Recently, Joost went with his parents and brother to a very special zoo in Arnhem. It has an enormous hall with a tropical rain forest inside, called the Bush. In the Bush you have to find your way through the dense jungle. You cross over streams on hanging bridges and crawl behind waterfalls on your hands and knees. Sometimes you have to run for cover from the tropical rains that suddenly fall from the sky.

Joost especially likes it that there are animals wandering around in the Bush that you would also find in a real rain forest. Fortunately, all the animals in the Bush are harmless. Otherwise, a trip through the rain forest might get a little too exciting.

Special days for the whole family

St. Nicholas' Eve: a special day for children

On 5 December, people in the Netherlands celebrate St. Nicholas' Eve. Children find it especially exciting, because they receive presents. They also eat a lot of sugary things, like spiced biscuits and sweets.

Usually you get a large piece of chocolate shaped like the first letter of your name.

Saint Nicholas was a bishop who did many good things for children a long time ago. In the Netherlands, little children believe Saint Nicholas really exists. They are told that he lives in Spain and has a big book with lists of naughty children and good ones.

Saint Nicholas comes to the Netherlands a couple of weeks before St. Nicholas' Eve. You can even see him arrive on television. He sails into the harbour on an old steamboat. After he comes ashore, he rides his white horse through the city. Thousands of children stand along his route with their parents. They all sing special songs for him. Saint Nicholas brings along his helpers, who are called *Zwarte Pieten*. They are people dressed up in colourful costumes with their faces painted black, who hand out sweets to children.

People often write poems to go along with their presents.
They also make funny packages with surprise gifts inside.

▼

fritters with raisins or apples in them. At midnight the fireworks begin. There are loud explosions everywhere. Everyone can see and hear that the new year has begun.

When Saint Nicholas is in the Netherlands, children leave their shoes next to the stove or the heating. They believe that Saint Nicholas rides across the rooftops at night on his white horse. His helpers climb down the chimney to put sweets or little presents into the children's shoes. Many children put a carrot in their shoes for Saint Nicholas' horse. Saint Nicholas is a bit like Santa Claus.

Other special days

At Easter, Dutch people eat lots of eggs. Children colour hard-boiled eggs. In the shops there are lots of chocolate eggs for sale, small ones and very big ones. And the parents hide real eggs or chocolate eggs in the house and the garden. The children have to hunt for them.

At Christmas many people have a Christmas tree. People spend Christmas Day and Boxing Day with their families, and they often give each other presents.

On New Year's Eve most children are allowed to stay up until after the clock strikes twelve. People often spend the evening with their friends and relatives. They eat apple turnovers and *oliebollen*, which are

"A Close Look at the Netherlands" is a publication of the Dutch Ministry of Foreign Affairs. This publication is part of an information package for young people developed in cooperation with the European Platform for Dutch Education.

Author
Gerda Telgenhof

Development and realisation
Wolters-Noordhoff bv, Groningen/Houten, the Netherlands

Coordination
International Information and Communication Division, Ministry of Foreign Affairs

Translation
Translation Department, Ministry of Foreign Affairs

Design
Frederike Bouten, Utrecht

Drawings
Helen van Vliet, Rotterdam: pp. 1, 4, 5, 7, 14, 15, 24, 30, 45, 51, 54
Ruud Bruijn, Krommenie-Zaanstad: pp. 6, 13, 31, 41
Fred Marschall, Amsterdam: pp. 9 top left, 28 (full page), 29
Frederike Bouten, Utrecht: p. 27
Mercis B.V., Amsterdam/Fotoarchief Dick Bruna: p. 36 bottom left.
Marcel Jurriëns, Boxtel: pp. 37, 59

Photographs
Benelux Press, Voorburg: pp. 4, 5, 8 bottom right, 12, 16, 18 (full page), 19, 22 bottom, 25, 30, 32, 33 bottom left, 34 bottom, 35 top, 43 top right, 46, 49 bottom left, 50 (full page), 55, 57 bottom.
BP, Voorburg / Paul C. Pet: p. 8 top left
BP, Voorburg / Dirk Visbach: pp. 9, 15
BP, Voorburg / Paul van Gaalen: p. 10
BP, Voorburg / Henk van der Leeden: pp. 11, 25 bottom right
BP, Voorburg / Igno Cuypers: p. 14
BP, Voorburg / Spaarnestad Fotoarchief, Haarlem: p. 21 bottom right
BP, Voorburg / Fotostock, Amsterdam: pp. 21 top, 51, 52, 58
BP, Voorburg / B&U, Amsterdam: pp. 22 top, 45, 59

BP, Voorburg / Stichting TongTong, Den Haag: p. 27
BP, Voorburg / Wim Hendriks: p. 35 bottom
BP, Voorburg / Rob Verhorst: p. 37 bottom
BP, Voorburg / AKG-photo, Berlin: pp. 38, 39 top
BP, Voorburg / Christies Images, London: p. 39 bottom
BP, Voorburg / ACZ, Gorkum: p. 48
BP, Voorburg / Porceleyne Fles, Delft: p. 49 top
BP, Voorburg / Yvonne Wacht: p. 56
BP, Voorburg / Burgers Zoo, Arnhem: p. 57 top
Ministry of Foreign Affairs, The Hague / Aeroview B.V.: p. 8 top right
Ministry of Foreign Affairs, The Hague / Aerocamera - Bart Hofmeester: p. 13
Ministry of Foreign Affairs, The Hague / P. Horree: pp. 17, 42 bottom left
Ministry of Foreign Affairs, The Hague : p. 33 top right
Ministry of Foreign Affairs, The Hague / KLM Aerocarto: pp. 42 top right, 43 top left
Ministry of Foreign Affairs, The Hague / Vincent van Zeijst: p. 43 bottom.
Ministry of Foreign Affairs, The Hague / Publiciteitsfotografie B.V.: p. 44 top right
Foto Plus +, Laren: p. 20
Catchlight, Huizen: pp. 23, 26, 53
Government Information Service, The Hague: p. 34 top
Anne Frank Stichting, Amsterdam: p. 36
Royal Concertgebouw Orchestra, Amsterdam: p. 37 top
Shell Photo Service, Rotterdam: p. 40 (full page)
E. van Leeuwarden, Rotterdam: p. 47

First English-language edition, 2000
ISBN 90 5328 125 8

15673